CLAUDIA THE CRAB'S BIG FIGHT

Published in 2017 by Douglass Day
http://www.douglassday.com

First printed in 2017
Copyright ©
Dan Douglass has asserted his right under the Copyright, Designs, and Patents Act 1988 to be identified as the author of this work.

All rights reserved. No part of this publication may be reproduced or transmitted in any form or by any means, electronic or mechanical including photocopy, recording or any information storage and retrieval system, without prior permission in writing from the publisher.

A catalogue record for this book is available from the British Library.

Paperback
978-0-9957588-2-7

Hardback

Printed and bound by Pureprint Group.

TWO

TALES FROM THE SEABED

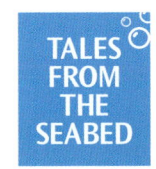

Claudia the crab's big fight

BY DAN DOUGLASS

STORY BY: DAN DOUGLASS

ILLUSTRATIONS BY: SUSAN BATORI

DESIGN BY: DAVID PENN

Have you heard of a boxing crab?
It's strange, I quite agree.
There are boxing kangaroos on land
But they never go in the sea.

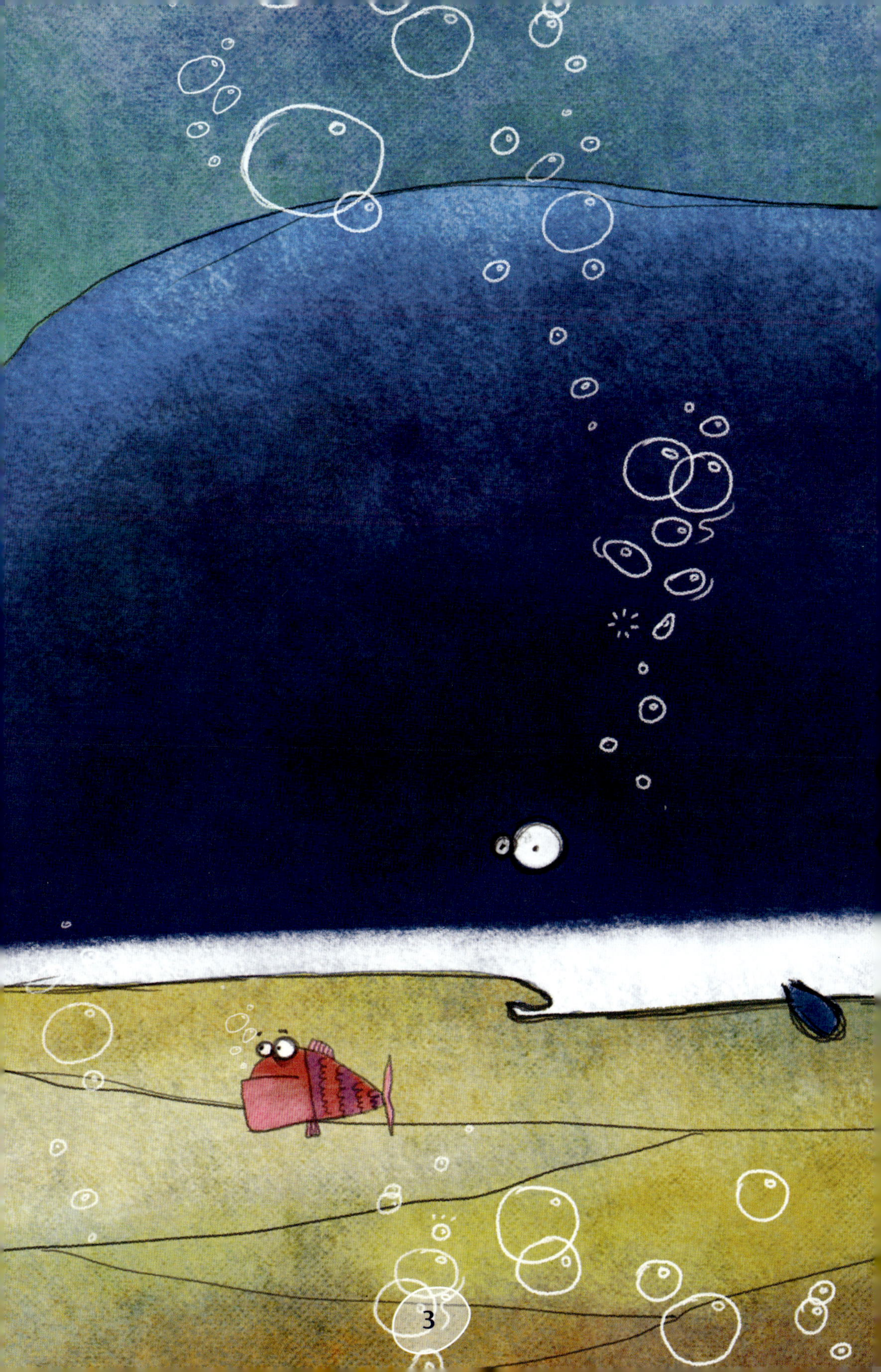

Well, here's one I can name
He's a crab called Buster Jaw.
And his biggest claim to fame?
He's got just the one left claw.

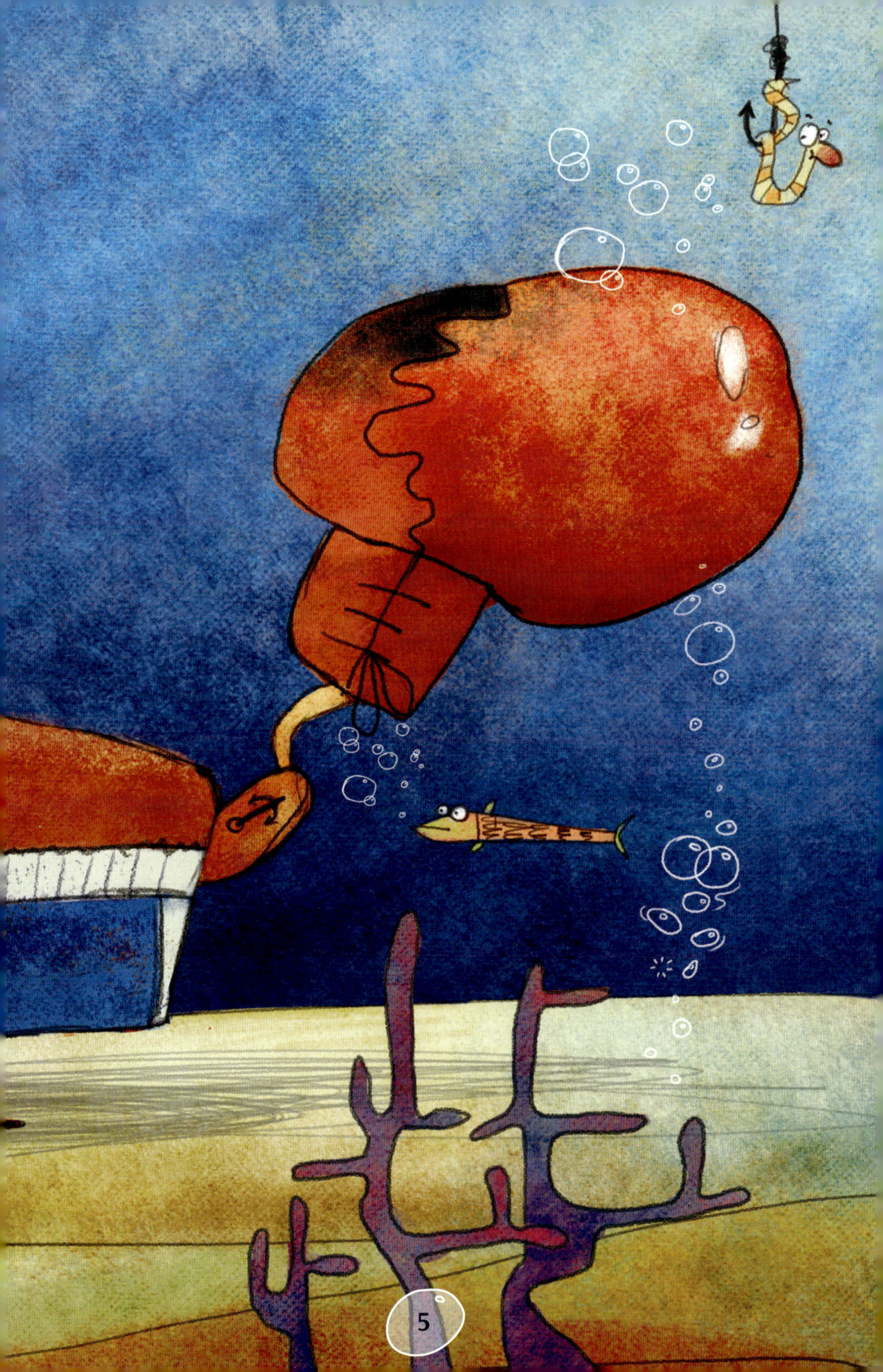

He trains up beginners
In his seaside rock pool gym.
He turns them into winners
And they owe it all to him.

7

One day, as he sparred with a cod
A crab stopped him for a chat.
She told him she was Claudia
But there was more to her
than that.

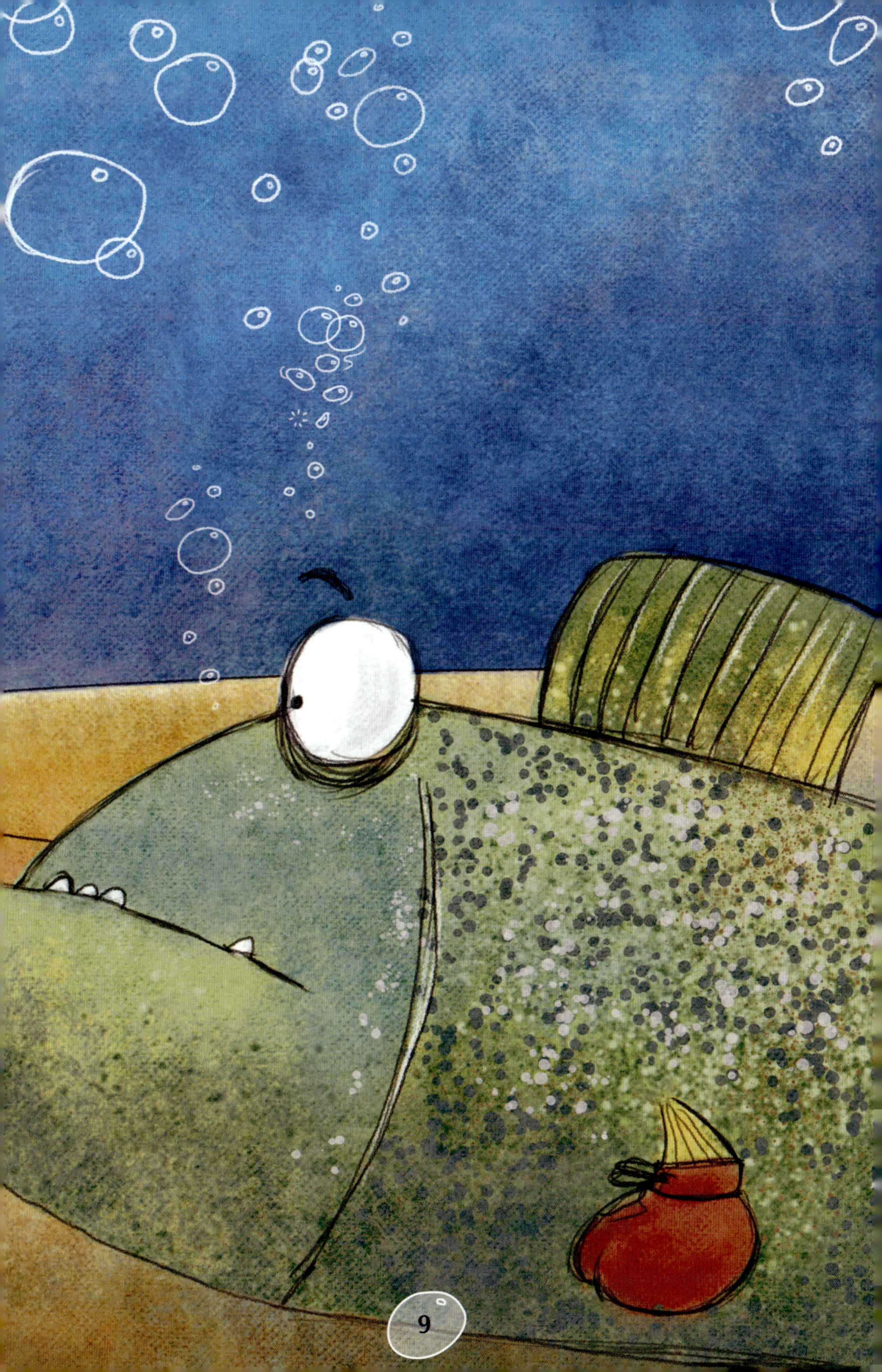

"I'm a boxing crab," she said.
Buster laughed, amazed.
"I've never seen a female fight
In all my boxing days."

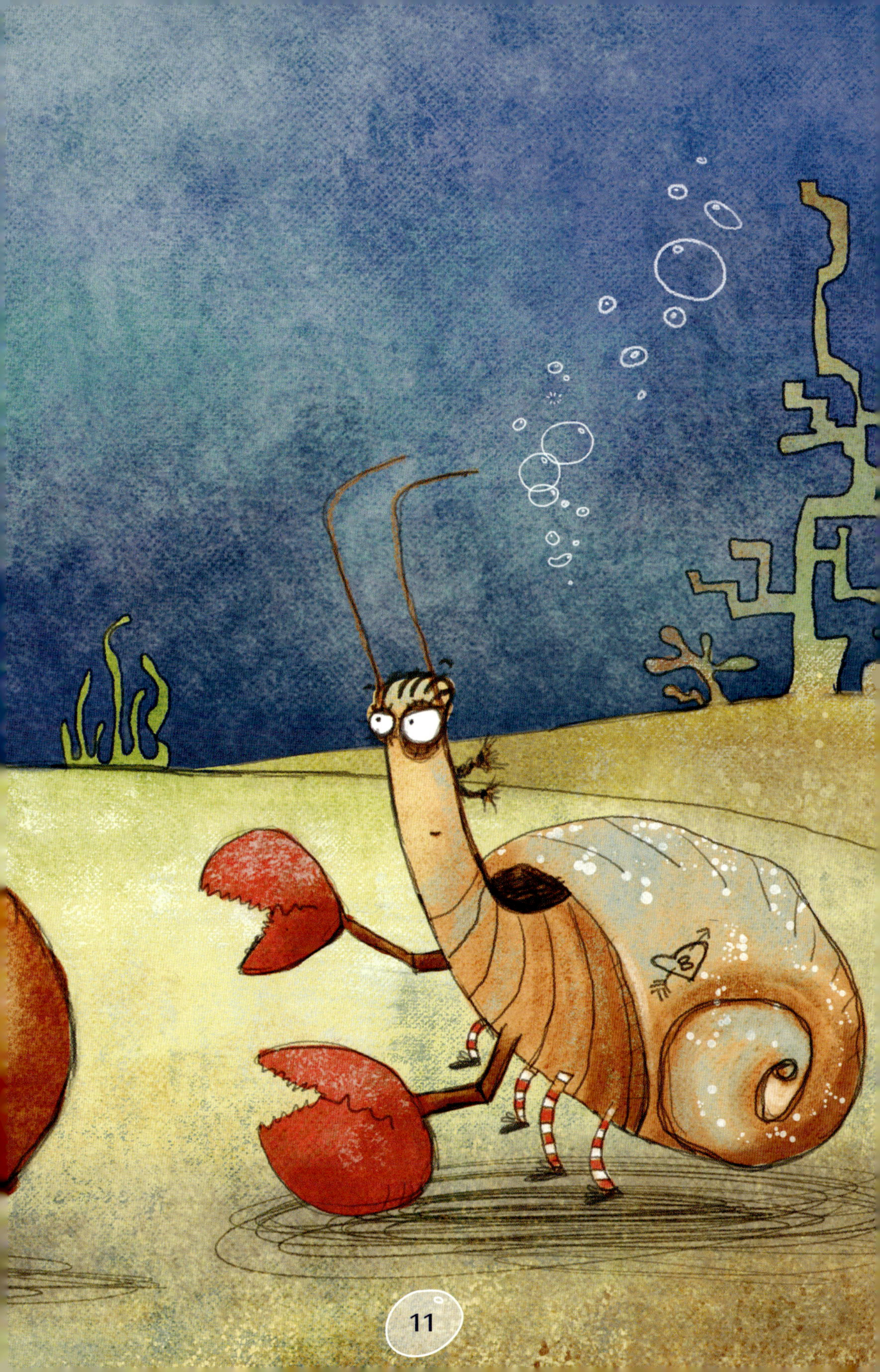

Showing him her
mighty swing
She clenched her tiny claw
And punched so hard with the thing
He dropped straight to the floor.

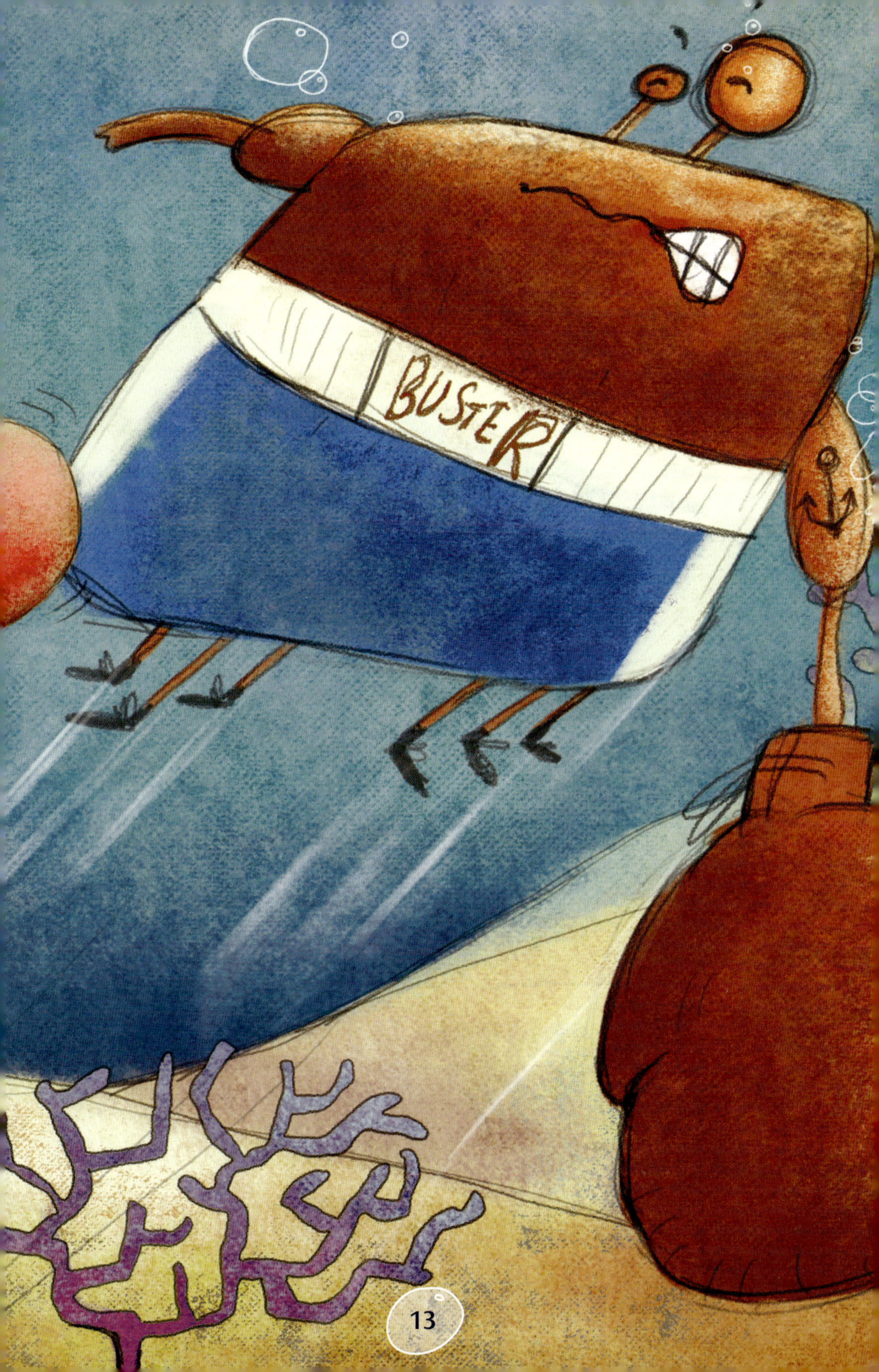
BUSTER

So Buster gave her the chance
To train hard all the hours
To lift and skip and punch and dance
And show her boxing powers.

15

One day a crayfish, named Rock Slim
And something of a bruiser
Challenged her to box with him
By shouting out, "You loser!"

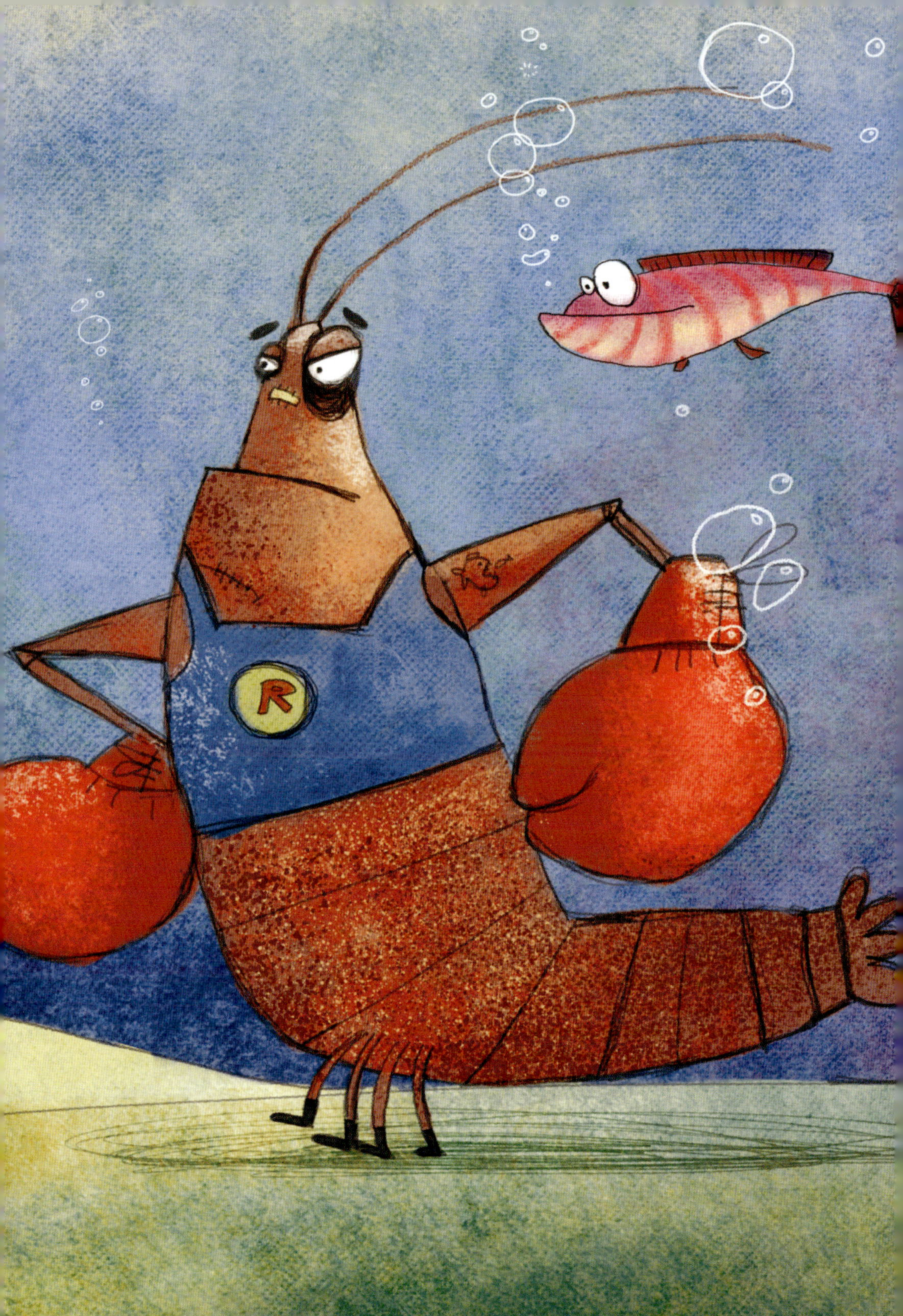
R

She punched him so hard on his chin
One swing and he was out
For Claudia always fought to win.
Of that there was no doubt.

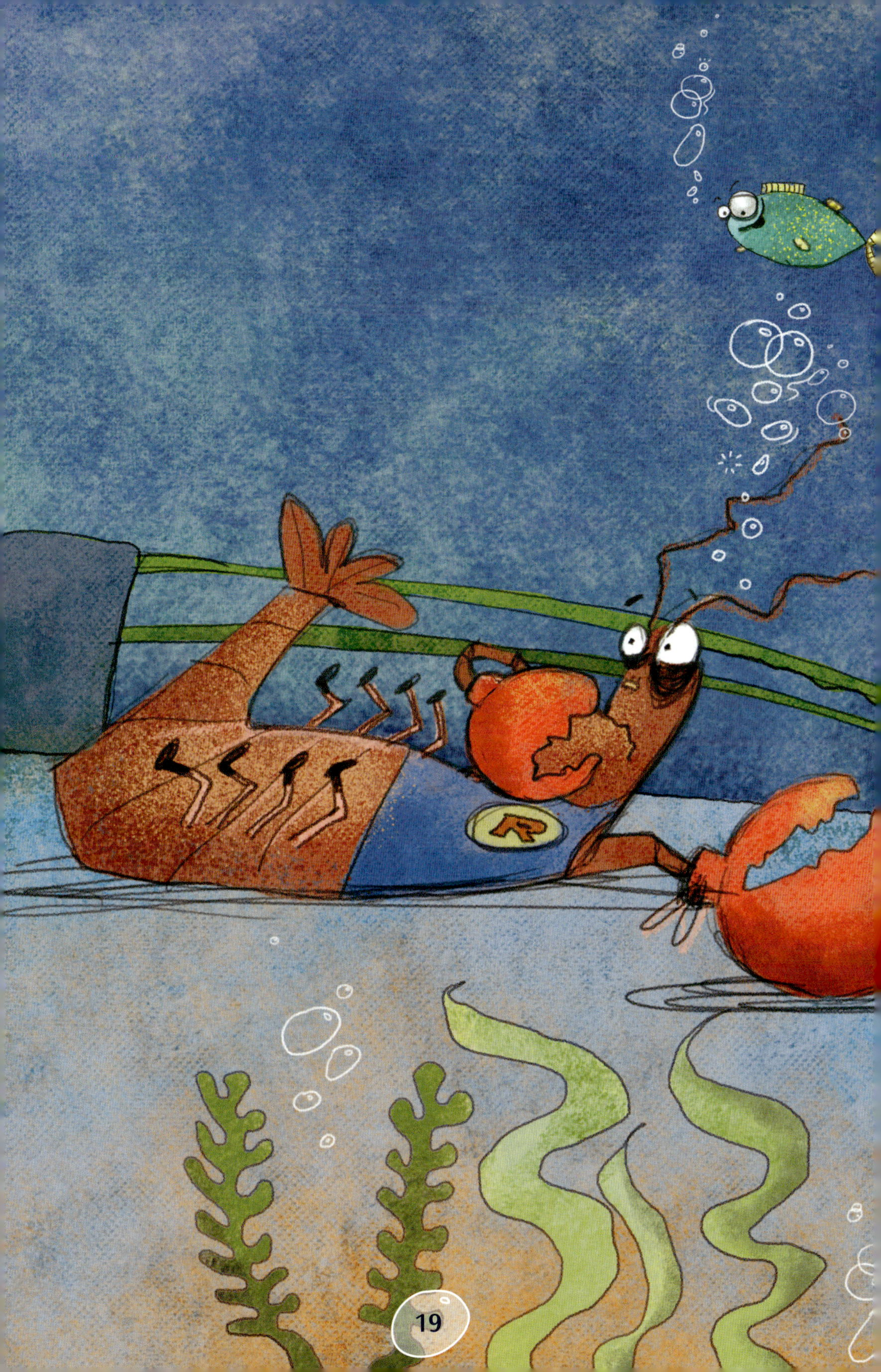

The crayfish nursed his broken head. "Well, who would have guessed you'd be my champion?" Buster said "You can out-box all the rest."

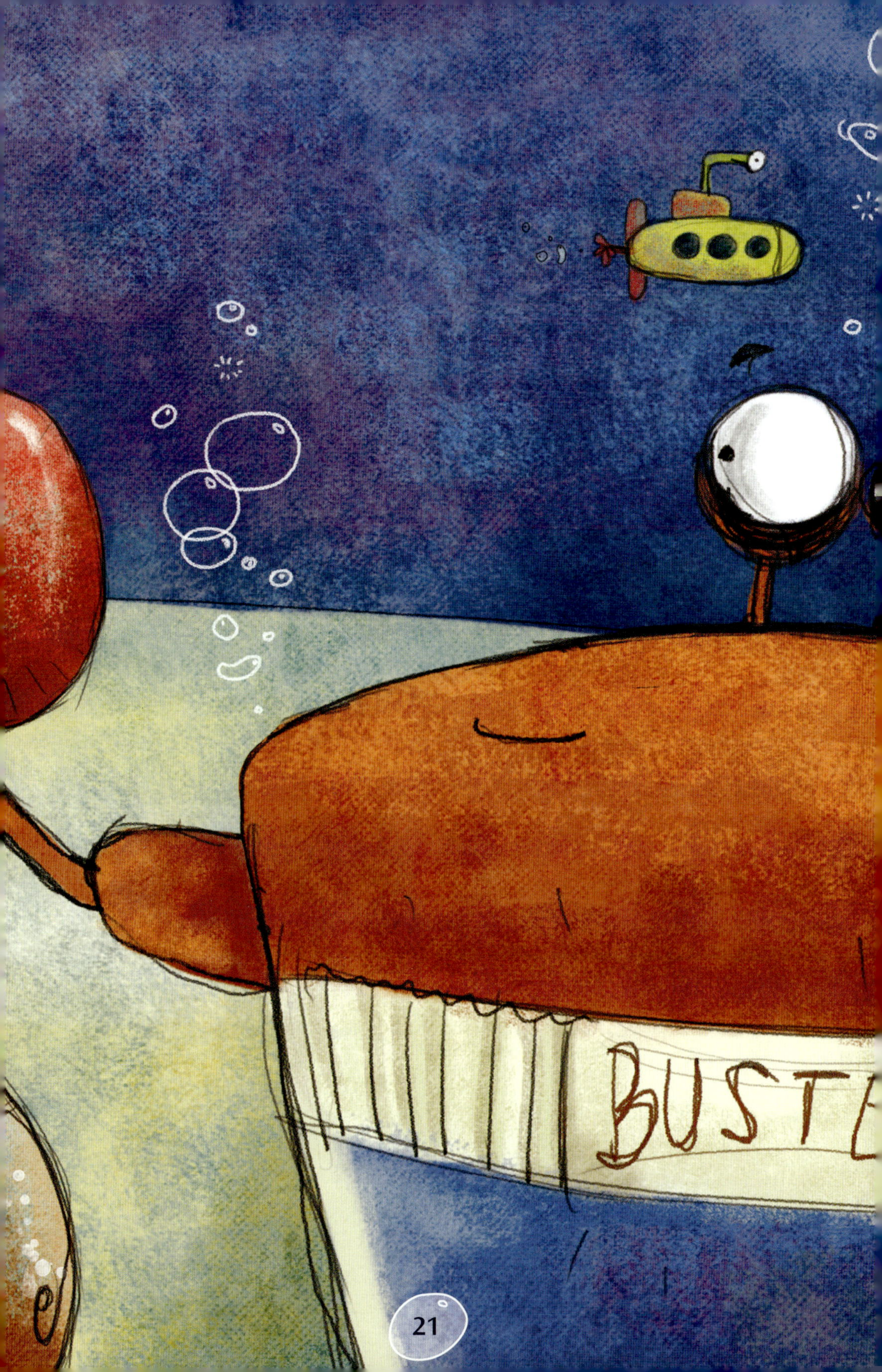
BUSTE

To lift the crown, Claudia had to beat
John Dory, a heavyweight slugger
Whose lobster trainer loved to cheat
And so had planned to drug her.

He placed a puffer's poisoned barb
In big John Dory's fin
So one big swish from the fish
Would make her small head spin.

24

The big day came and creatures swam
From all the seven seas
To see Claudia the boxing crab
Bring John Dory to his knees.

John Dory swept into the ring
As if he owned the place.
He had a big crab-eating grin
On his big bad scaly face.

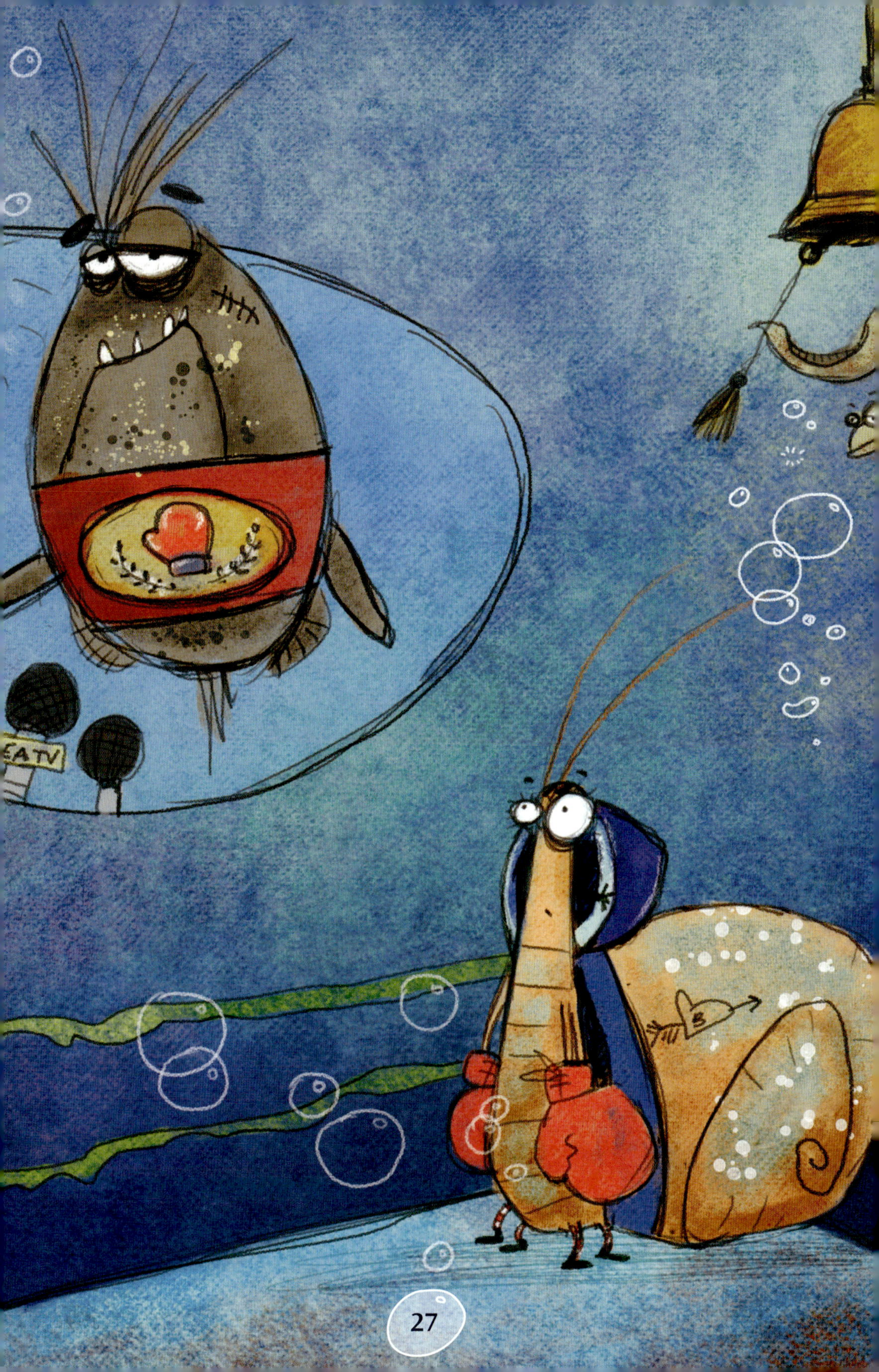
EATV

One swipe of Big John's tail
knocked poor Claudia out
And the referee soon called an end
To this sad world title bout.

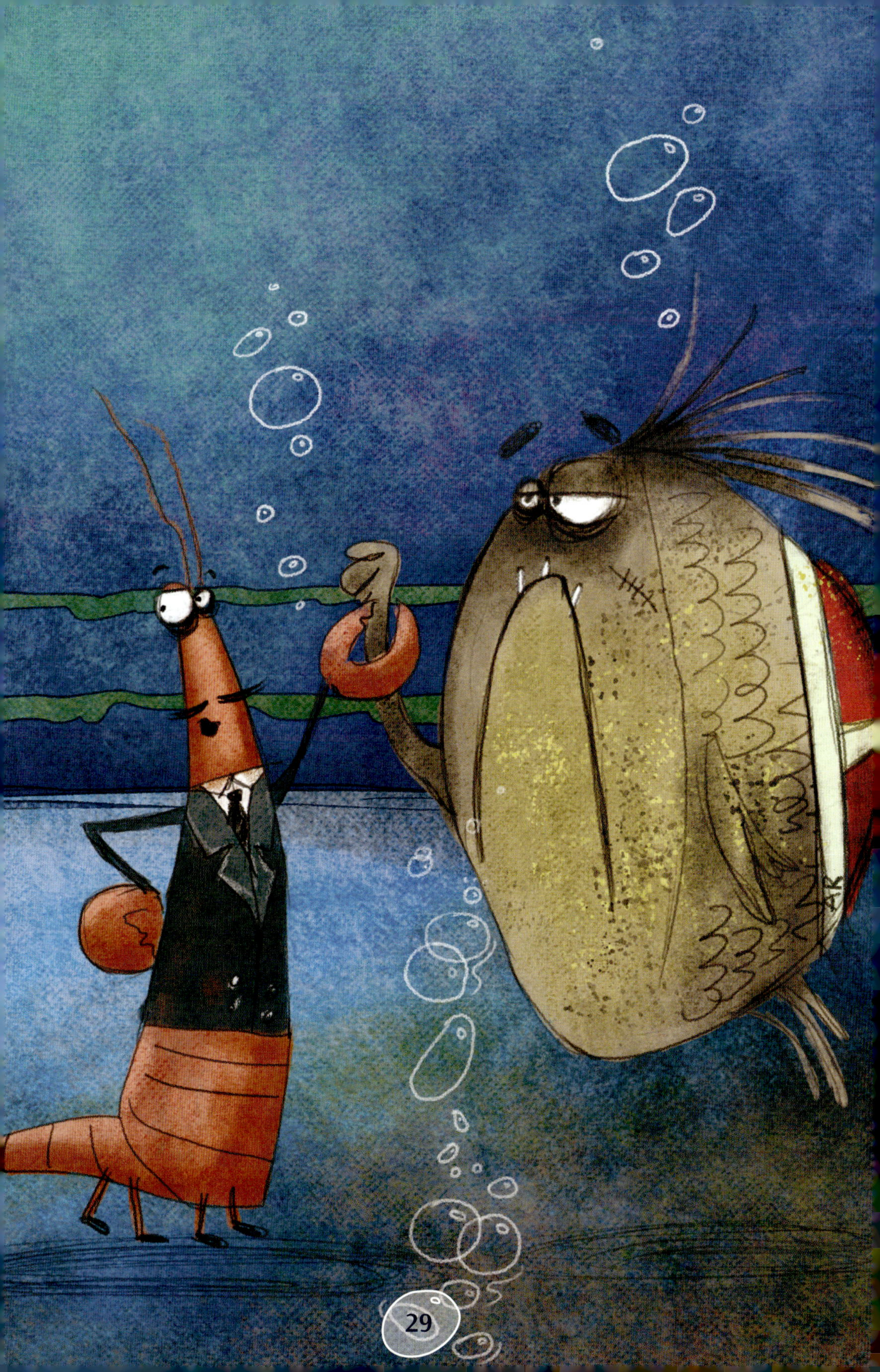

"John Dory, attaboy!"
His coach was heard to say
And the cheating duo jumped for joy
In a most unsporting way.

Poisoned by the cheating fish
Her life was now the prize
But Buster held her in his claws
And she opened her tiny eyes.

"Look," she shouted to the crowd
And pointed to Big John's tail
"Cheating in the ring is not allowed.
I was set up to fail."

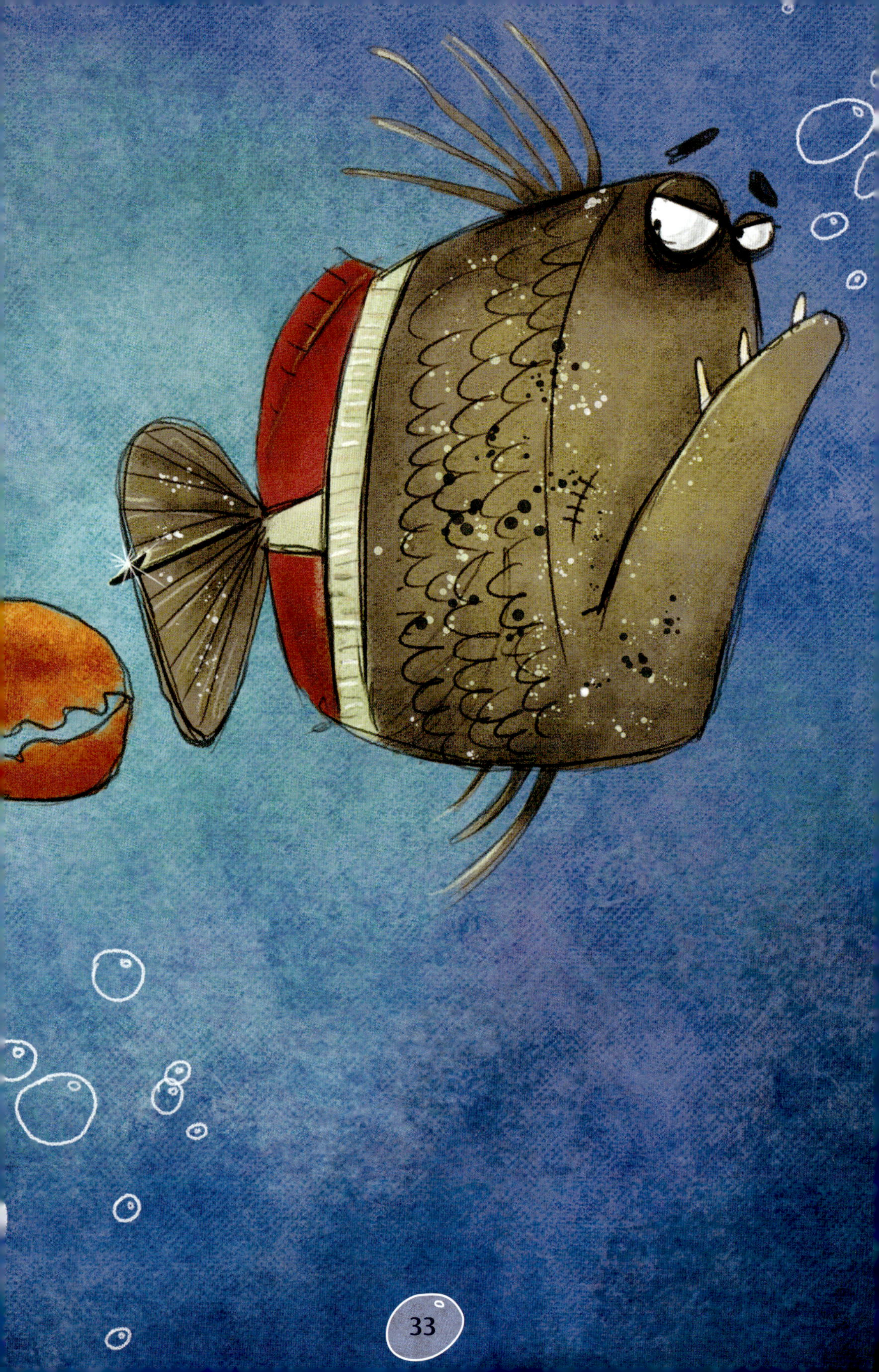

Claudia rose up to her feet
And gave John such a clout
He flew into a ringside seat
And his poisoned barb fell out.

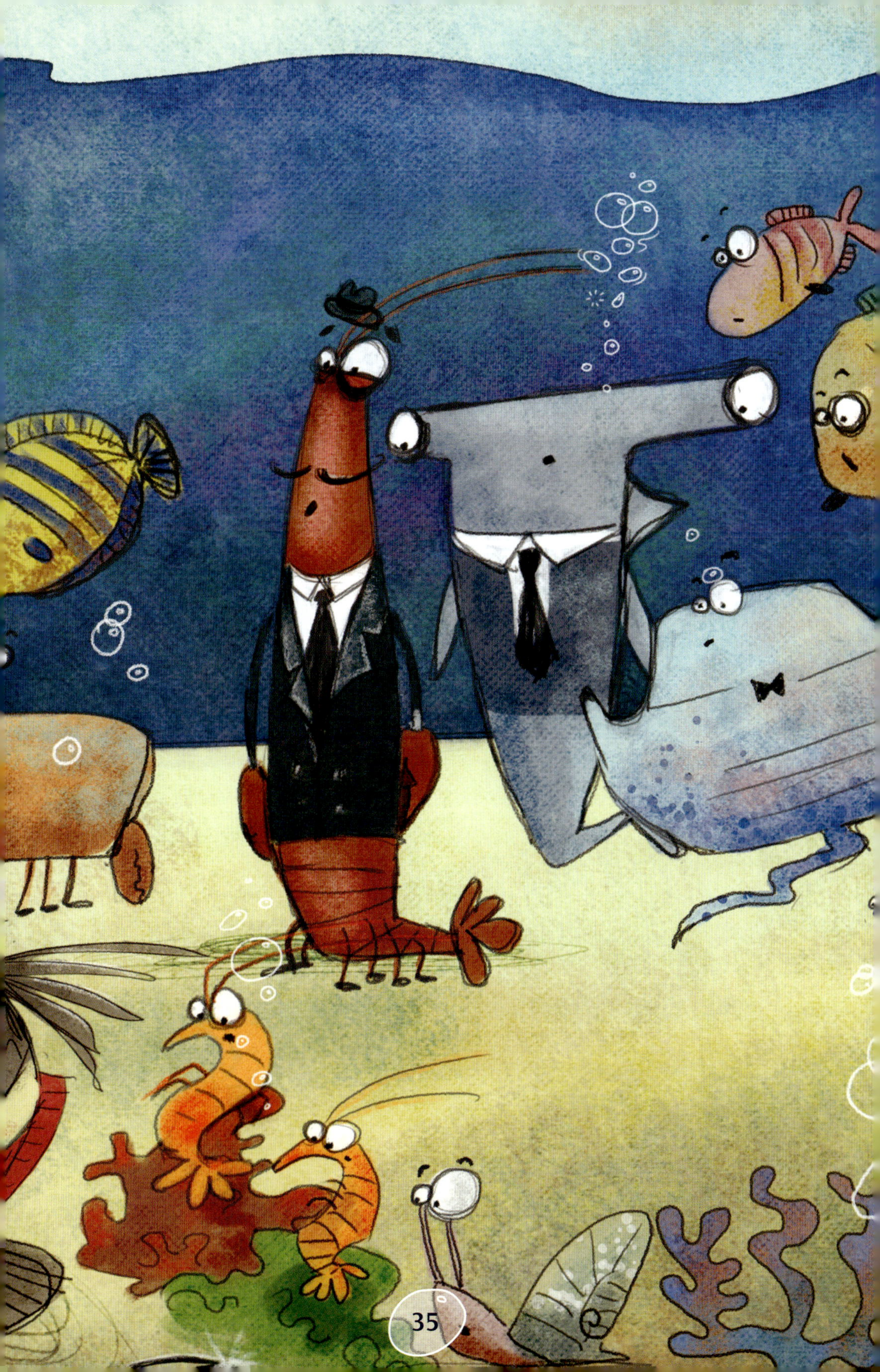

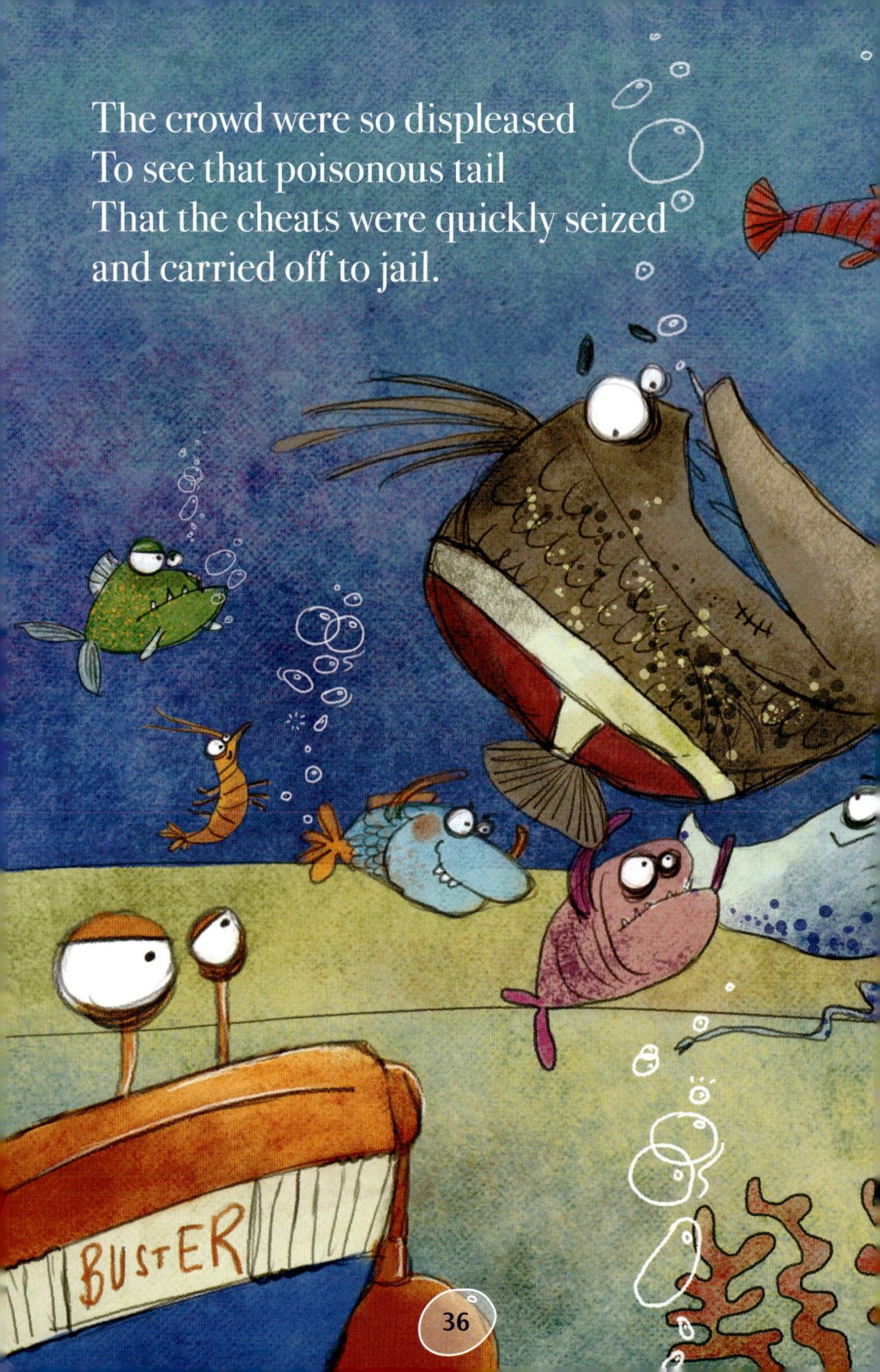

The crowd were so displeased
To see that poisonous tail
That the cheats were quickly seized
and carried off to jail.

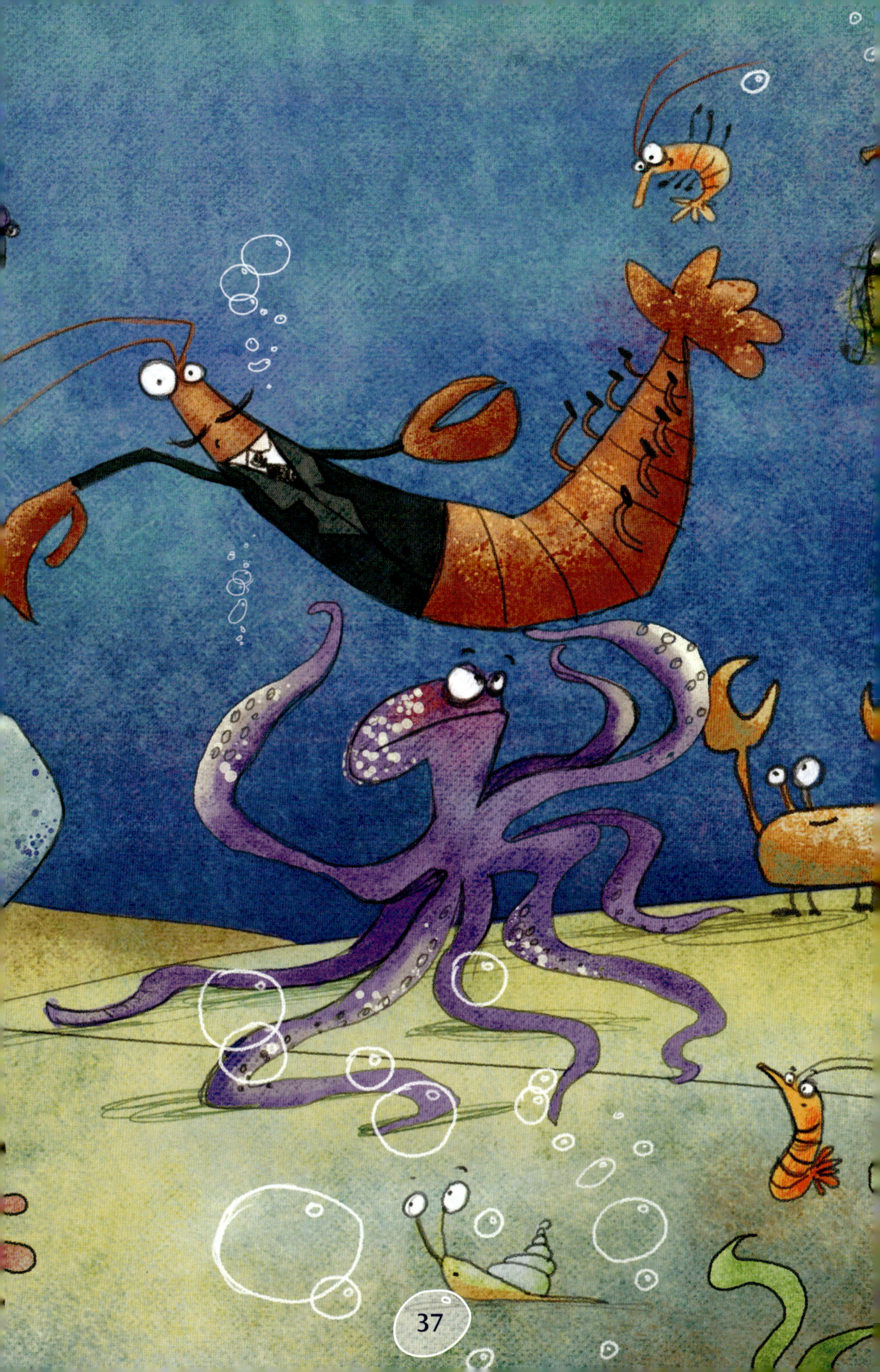

Buster crowned her boxing queen.
Now they run the gym together.
It's the greatest love match ever seen.
This one will last forever.

She kept her crown through many fights.
Fifteen bouts, fifteen KO's.
Her title is now hers by rights,
As every sea bass knows.

And now throughout the rock pools,
All the sea life tells the story
Of how a tiny hermit crab
Came to beat a big John Dory.

LIVE AT THE SAND

CLAUDIA THE CRAB
vs
BIG JOHN DORY

ERNIE THE SLIPPERY EEL
vs
GIANT SID THE AMAZING SQUID

SHRIMPY JIM
vs
TIDDLER PETE

for the flyweight title
promoted by Louie the lobster

Dan Douglass

Dan Douglass works as an Executive Creative Director in advertising and lives in London.

After graduating in English from Oxford, he joined a London agency as an Account Executive, but soon realised he'd rather be telling stories on behalf of brands than carrying them as the contents of art-bags. So he became a copywriter and never looked back.

'Tales from the Seabed' is his second collection of children's stories after 'Bees, Bugs and Grubs' Tales' and 'Tales for the Birds'.

Other stories from this author:

How Terry saved the termite city

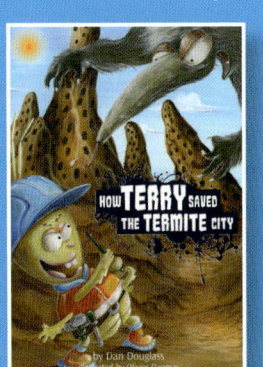

Eartha's story - how the worm turned

How Boris got his buzz back

Raymondo the Ray's incredible magic trick

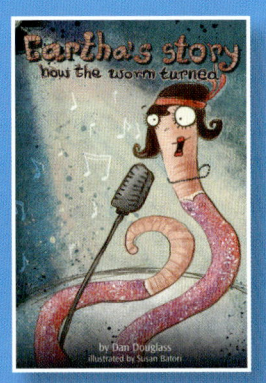

Dave the dolphin's good day

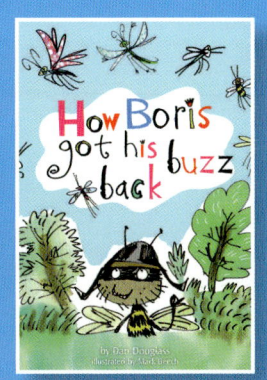

Two toucans can

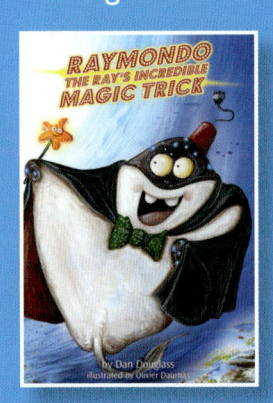

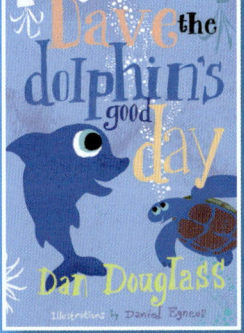

The oh so so-so kakapo

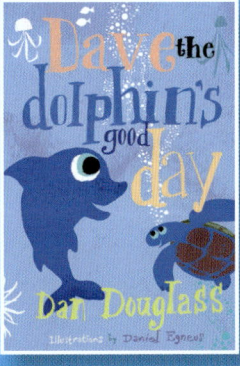

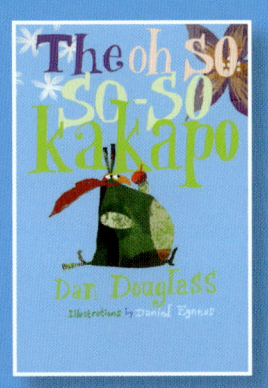

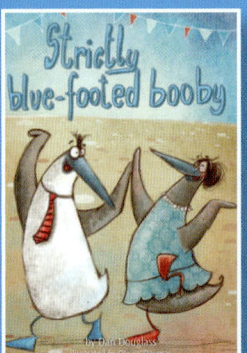

Strictly blue-footed booby